Silly Snacks & Classroom Treats

Publications International, Ltd.

Favorite Brand Name Recipes at www.fbnr.com

Microwave Cooking: Microwave ovens vary in wattage. Use the cooking times as guidelines and check for doneness before adding more time.

Preparation/Cooking Times: Preparation times are based on the approximate amount of time required to assemble the recipe before cooking, baking, chilling or serving. These times include preparation steps such as measuring, chopping and mixing. The fact that some preparations and cooking can be done simultaneously is taken into account. Preparation of optional ingredients and serving suggestions is not included.

Contents

Go with the Punches

Bobbing Head Punch

Assorted candies
Assorted fruit slices and pieces
Water
6 cups white grape juice
4 cups ginger ale
2 cups apple juice or 2 additional cups ginger ale
Green food coloring

1. Arrange candy and fruit slices in bottom of 9-inch glass pie plate to create a face. (Remember, the bottom of the face is what will show in the punch bowl.)

2. Add water to cover face; carefully place in freezer. Freeze overnight.

3. At time of serving, add ginger ale and juices to 4- to 5-quart punch bowl. Tint mixture green. Invert pie plate, placing one hand underneath; run under cold running water to release frozen face. Place ice mold upside down on top of juice mixture; serve. *Makes 20 cups*

Festive Citrus Punch

I can (6 ounces) frozen Florida grapefruit juice concentrate, thawed

I can (6 ounces) frozen pineapple juice concentrate, thawed

I cup water

3 tablespoons honey

2 tablespoons grenadine syrup* (optional)

I bottle (I liter) ginger ale, chilled

Mint sprigs for garnish (optional)

Ice cubes

Grenadine may contain alcohol, so be sure to check the label before using.

Combine grapefruit juice, pineapple juice, water and honey in punch bowl or large pitcher. Stir in grenadine, if desired. Stir until well combined.

Just before serving, slowly pour ginger ale down side of punch bowl. Stir gently to combine. Garnish, if desired. Serve over ice in chilled glasses.

Makes about 18 (4-ounce) servings

Favorite recipe from **Florida Department of Citrus**

Cranberry Snow Punch

I cup apple juice, chilled

½ cup superfine sugar

1½ cups cranberry juice cocktail, chilled

1½ cups bitter lemon or tonic water, chilled

I pint vanilla frozen yogurt

1. Combine apple juice and sugar in punch bowl; stir until sugar dissolves. Stir in cranberry juice and bitter lemon.

2. Scoop frozen yogurt onto top of punch. Serve immediately.

Makes 8 servings (about 4 ounces each)

Handy Fruit Punch

Ingredients
   Green food coloring
   I envelope (4 ounces) orange-flavored presweetened drink mix
   I can (12 ounces) frozen lemonade concentrate, thawed
   I bottle (2 liters) ginger ale

Supplies
   I new plastic household glove

1. One day ahead, fill pitcher with 3 cups water; tint with green food coloring. Pour into glove; tightly secure top of glove with twist tie. Line baking sheet with paper towels; place glove on prepared baking sheet. Use inverted custard cup to elevate tied end of glove to prevent leaking. Freeze overnight.

2. When ready to serve, combine drink mix, lemonade concentrate and 4 cups water in large bowl; stir until drink mix is dissolved and mixture is well blended. Pour into punch bowl; add ginger ale.

3. Cut glove away from ice; float frozen hand in punch.

Makes 16 (6-ounce) servings and 1 ice hand

Pineapple Raspberry Punch

5 cups DOLE® Pineapple Juice
I quart raspberry cranberry drink
I pint fresh or frozen raspberries
I lemon, thinly sliced
   Ice

• Chill ingredients. Combine in punch bowl.   *Makes 9 cups*

Spiced Cranberry Punch

2 cups **KARO®** Light Corn Syrup
¼ cup water
6 cinnamon sticks
2 tablespoons whole cloves
½ teaspoon ground allspice
2 quarts cranberry juice, chilled
1 quart orange juice, chilled
1 can (46 ounces) pineapple juice, chilled
2 quarts ginger ale, chilled
½ cup lemon juice

1. In medium saucepan combine corn syrup, water, cinnamon sticks, cloves and allspice. Bring to boil over medium-high heat. Reduce heat; simmer 10 minutes.

2. Cover and refrigerate until thoroughly chilled; strain to remove spices.

3. Just before serving, combine spiced syrup, fruit juices, ginger ale and lemon juice.   *Makes about 36 (6-ounce) servings*

Prep Time: 15 minutes, plus chilling

"Lemon Float" Punch

Juice of 10 to 12 **SUNKIST®** lemons (2 cups)
¾ cup sugar
4 cups water
1 bottle (2 liters) ginger ale, chilled
1 pint lemon sherbet or frozen vanilla yogurt
Lemon half-cartwheel slices and fresh mint leaves for garnish

Combine lemon juice and sugar; stir to dissolve sugar. Add water; chill. To serve, in large punch bowl, combine lemon mixture and ginger ale. Add small scoops of sherbet, lemon slices and mint.

Makes about 15 cups (thirty 6-ounce servings)

Creepy Crawler Punch

1 **Creepy Crawler Ice Ring (recipe follows)**
2 **cups corn syrup**
¼ **cup water**
6 **cinnamon sticks**
2 **tablespoons whole cloves**
½ **teaspoon ground allspice**
8 **cups (64 ounces) cranberry juice cocktail**
4 **cups (32 ounces) orange juice**
6 **cups (48 ounces) pineapple juice**
½ **cup lemon juice**
8 **cups ginger ale**

1. Prepare Creepy Crawler Ice Ring.

2. Cook and stir corn syrup and water in medium saucepan over medium-high heat. Add cinnamon sticks, cloves and allspice; stir gently. Bring to a boil and immediately reduce heat to a simmer; simmer 10 minutes.

3. Refrigerate, covered, until chilled. Remove cinnamon sticks and discard. Strain out cloves and discard.

4. In punch bowl, combine syrup mixture with juices and ginger ale. Unmold Creepy Crawler Ice Ring; add to punch bowl.

Makes 36 servings

Creepy Crawler Ice Ring

1 **cup gummy worms or other creepy crawler candy**
4 **cups lemon-lime thirst quencher beverage**

- Arrange gummy worms in bottom of 5-cup ring mold; fill mold with thirst quencher beverage. Freeze until solid, 8 hours or overnight.

Holiday Citrus Punch

Ingredients

    I pint vanilla frozen yogurt, softened

      Fresh or frozen raspberries

    I can (12 ounces) frozen lemonade concentrate, thawed

    I can (12 ounces) frozen orange-cranberry juice concentrate, thawed

    I can (12 ounces) frozen **Ruby Red** grapefruit juice concentrate, thawed

    2 cups cold water

    ¼ cup lime juice

    2 bottles (28 ounces each) ginger ale, chilled

Supplies

    Parchment paper

    Assorted cookie cutters in star, snowflake or holiday shapes

1. Line 9-inch square baking dish with parchment paper. Spread yogurt evenly into prepared dish; freeze until firm. Meanwhile, place baking sheet in freezer to chill.

2. Remove frozen yogurt from baking pan. Using cookie cutters, cut out desired shapes from frozen yogurt. Transfer cutouts to chilled baking sheet. Press raspberry into center of each yogurt cutout; freeze until ready to serve.

3. Combine fruit juice concentrates, water and lime juice in punch bowl. Just before serving, pour in ginger ale. Float yogurt cutouts in punch.

Makes 24 to 26 servings

Golden Harvest Punch

    4 cups **MOTT'S®** Apple Juice

    4 cups orange juice

    3 liters club soda

    I quart orange sherbet

    5 pound bag ice cubes (optional)

Combine apple juice, orange juice and club soda in punch bowl. Add scoops of sherbet or ice, if desired.

Makes 25 servings

Desert Thirst Punch with Red Eye Cubes

 2 cups sugar
 1 cup water
 ¼ cup grated fresh ginger
 Rind of 1 lemon, cut into strips
 ¾ cup fresh lemon juice (juice of 5 or 6 lemons)
 7½ cups club soda, chilled
 Lemon slices for garnish
 Red Eye Cubes (recipe follows)

1. Prepare Red Eye Cubes.

2. Combine sugar, water, ginger and lemon rind in medium saucepan. Bring to a boil. Reduce heat to low; simmer 5 minutes or until sugar dissolves and becomes syrupy. Set aside; cool completely. Stir in lemon juice and chill until serving time.

3. Strain 2½ cups lemon juice mixture into 1-quart measuring cup.

4. For punch, pour lemon syrup into large bowl. Add club soda; stir briefly. For individual servings, combine ¼ cup lemon syrup and ¾ cup club soda. Add 1 or 2 Red Eye Cubes; garnish with lemon slice.   *Makes 10 servings*

Red Eye Cubes

 Maraschino cherries or red seedless grapes

1. Fill ice cube tray half full with water. Freeze 30 minutes or until water just begins to solidify.

2. Place 1 cherry in center of each ice cube; cover with more water. Return to freezer for 2 hours or until solid.   *Makes about 14 cubes*

13

Citrus Sunrise Punch

8 thick slices cucumber
4 cups pineapple juice
1 cup orange juice
2 cups ginger ale
  Ice
8 tablespoons grenadine syrup*

Grenadine may contain alcohol, so be sure to check the label before using.

1. Cut cucumber slices into decorative shapes.

2. Combine pineapple and orange juices in large pitcher. Refrigerate until serving time.

3. Immediately before serving, stir ginger ale into juices. Fill glasses generously with ice and add cucumber shapes to rims. Pour punch into ice-filled glasses. Slowly drizzle 1 tablespoon grenadine over top of each serving.

Makes 8 servings

Strawberry Splash Punch

1½ cups fresh whole strawberries
  ½ cup lemon juice from concentrate, chilled
    1 (14-ounce) can EAGLE BRAND® Sweetened Condensed Milk (NOT evaporated milk), chilled
    1 (1-liter) bottle strawberry-flavored carbonated beverage, chilled
    Ice cubes, if desired
    Fresh whole strawberries, if desired

1. In blender container, combine 1½ cups strawberries and lemon juice; cover and blend until smooth.

2. Add Eagle Brand; cover and blend. Pour into large pitcher. Gradually stir in carbonated beverage. Add ice, if desired. Garnish each serving with whole strawberry, if desired.

Makes 10 servings

Prep Time: 10 minutes

Festive Cranberry Cream Punch

Cranberry Ice Ring (recipe follows) or ice
1 (14-ounce) can EAGLE BRAND® Sweetened Condensed Milk (NOT evaporated milk)
1 (12-ounce) can frozen cranberry juice cocktail concentrate, thawed
Red food coloring, if desired
2 (1-liter) bottles club soda or ginger ale, chilled

1. Prepare Cranberry Ice Ring one day in advance.

2. In punch bowl, combine Eagle Brand, concentrate and food coloring, if desired.

3. Just before serving, add club soda and Cranberry Ice Ring or ice. Store tightly covered in refrigerator.   *Makes about 3 quarts*

Cranberry Ice Ring

2 cups cranberry juice cocktail
1½ cups water
¾ to 1 cup cranberries and lime slices or mint leaves

1. Combine cranberry juice cocktail and water. In 1½-quart ring mold, pour ½ cup cranberry liquid.

2. Arrange cranberries and lime slices or mint leaves in mold; freeze.

3. Add remaining 3 cups cranberry liquid to mold; freeze overnight.
Makes 1 ice ring

Spiced Cider Punch (Goblin's Brew)

4 cups water
1 cup packed brown sugar
¾ cup granulated sugar
4 cinnamon sticks
¼ teaspoon whole cloves
4 cups freshly squeezed **SUNKIST®** orange juice
3 cups apple cider
Juice of 9 **SUNKIST®** lemons (1½ cups)
Whole cloves
Unpeeled **SUNKIST®** lemon cartwheel slices

In large saucepan, combine water, sugars, cinnamon and cloves. Bring to a boil, stirring to dissolve sugars. Reduce heat; simmer 5 minutes. Remove cinnamon and cloves. Add orange juice, cider and lemon juice; heat. Garnish with clove-studded lemon cartwheels.

Makes 13 cups (twenty-six ½-cup servings)

Christmas Carol Punch

2 medium red apples
2 quarts clear apple cider
½ cup **SUN•MAID®** Raisins
8 cinnamon sticks
2 teaspoons whole cloves
¼ cup lemon juice
Lemon slices
Orange slices

Core apples; slice into ½-inch rings. In Dutch oven, combine cider, apple rings, raisins, cinnamon and cloves. Bring to a boil over high heat; reduce heat to low and simmer 5 to 8 minutes or until apples are just tender. Remove cloves; add lemon juice, lemon slices and orange slices. Pour into punch bowl. Ladle into large mugs, include apple ring, raisins and citrus slices in each serving. Serve with spoons. *Makes about 8 cups*

Crazy Cupcakes

Stars and Stripes Cupcakes

42 cupcakes, any flavor
2 containers (16 ounces each) vanilla frosting
Fresh blueberries, washed and dried
Fresh strawberries, washed, dried, trimmed and halved

1. Frost cupcakes with vanilla frosting.

2. Decorate 9 cupcakes with blueberries, leaving space between blueberries. Decorate top halves of remaining cupcakes with strawberry halves.

3. Arrange cupcakes on rectangular tray or on table to form U.S. flag. Place blueberry-topped cupcakes in upper left part of tray and strawberry-topped cupcakes in rows to resemble red and white stripes of flag.

Makes 42 cupcakes

Chocolate Frosted Peanut Butter Cupcakes

⅓ cup butter, softened
⅓ cup creamy or chunky peanut butter
½ cup granulated sugar
¼ cup packed brown sugar
2 eggs
1 teaspoon vanilla
1¾ cups all-purpose flour
1½ teaspoons baking powder
¼ teaspoon salt
1¼ cups milk
Peanut Butter Chocolate Frosting (recipe follows)

1. Preheat oven to 350°F. Line 18 (2½-inch) muffin cups with foil baking cups.

2. Beat butter and peanut butter in large bowl with electric mixer at medium speed until smooth; beat in sugars until well mixed. Beat in eggs and vanilla.

3. Combine flour, baking powder and salt in medium bowl. Add flour mixture to peanut butter mixture alternately with milk, beginning and ending with flour mixture.

4. Pour batter into prepared muffin cups. Bake 23 to 25 minutes or until cupcakes spring back when touched and toothpicks inserted in centers come out clean. Cool in pans on wire racks 10 minutes; remove from pans and cool completely.

5. Prepare Peanut Butter Chocolate Frosting. Frost each cupcake with about 1½ tablespoons frosting. Garnish as desired.　　*Makes 18 cupcakes*

Peanut Butter Chocolate Frosting

4 cups powdered sugar
⅓ cup unsweetened cocoa powder
4 to 5 tablespoons milk, divided
3 tablespoons creamy peanut butter

Combine powdered sugar, cocoa, 4 tablespoons milk and peanut butter in large bowl. Beat with electric mixer at low speed until smooth. Beat in additional 1 tablespoon milk until of desired spreading consistency.

Makes about 2½ cups

Chocolate Frosted Peanut Butter Cupcakes

Easter Baskets and Bunnies Cupcakes

    2 cups sugar
1¾ cups all-purpose flour
    ¾ cup HERSHEY'S Cocoa or HERSHEY'S Dutch Processed
        Cocoa
1½ teaspoons baking powder
1½ teaspoons baking soda
    1 teaspoon salt
    2 eggs
    1 cup milk
    ½ cup vegetable oil
    2 teaspoons vanilla extract
    1 cup boiling water
    Creamy Vanilla Frosting (recipe follows)
    Green, red and yellow food color
3¾ cups MOUNDS® Sweetened Coconut Flakes, divided and
        tinted*
    Suggested garnishes (marshmallows, HERSHEY'S MINI
        KISSES™ Milk Chocolates, licorice, jelly beans)

To tint coconut, combine ¾ teaspoon water with several drops green food color in small bowl. Stir in 1¼ cups coconut. Toss with fork until evenly tinted. Repeat with red and yellow food color and remaining coconut.

1. Heat oven to 350°F. Line muffin cups (2½ inches in diameter) with paper bake cups.

2. Stir together sugar, flour, cocoa, baking powder, baking soda and salt in large bowl. Add eggs, milk, oil and vanilla; beat on medium speed of mixer 2 minutes. Stir in boiling water (batter will be thin). Fill muffin cups ⅔ full with batter.

3. Bake 22 to 25 minutes or until wooden pick inserted in center comes out clean. Cool completely. Prepare Creamy Vanilla Frosting; frost cupcakes. Immediately press desired color tinted coconut onto each cupcake. Garnish as desired to resemble Easter basket or bunny.

Makes about 33 cupcakes

Creamy Vanilla Frosting: Beat ⅓ cup softened butter or margarine in medium bowl. Add 1 cup powdered sugar and 1½ teaspoons vanilla extract; beat well. Add 2½ cups powdered sugar alternately with ¼ cup milk, beating to spreading consistency. Makes about 2 cups frosting.

Scarecrow Cupcakes

1¼ cups all-purpose flour
¾ teaspoon baking powder
½ teaspoon baking soda
¼ teaspoon salt
¾ teaspoon ground cinnamon
⅛ teaspoon *each* ground cloves, ground nutmeg and ground
    allspice
¾ cup heavy cream
2 tablespoons molasses
¼ cup butter, softened
¼ cup *each* granulated sugar and packed brown sugar
2 eggs
½ teaspoon vanilla
¾ cup sweetened shredded coconut
    Maple Frosting (page 28)
    **Toasted coconut, chow mein noodles, shredded wheat cereal,
    assorted candies and decorating gel**

1. Preheat oven to 350°F. Line 18 (2¾-inch) muffin cups with paper baking cups. Combine flour, baking powder, baking soda, salt and spices in medium bowl; set aside. Combine cream and molasses in small bowl; set aside.

2. Beat butter in large bowl until creamy. Add granulated sugar and brown sugar; beat until light and fluffy. Add eggs, one at a time, beating well after each addition. Blend in vanilla.

3. Add flour mixture alternately with cream mixture, beating well after each addition. Stir in coconut; spoon batter into prepared muffin cups, filling about half full.

4. Bake 20 to 25 minutes or until toothpick inserted in centers comes out clean. Cool in pan on wire racks 10 minutes. Remove cupcakes to racks; cool completely.

5. Prepare Maple Frosting. Frost cupcakes and decorate to make scarecrow faces as shown in photo. *Makes 18 cupcakes*

Tip: To make a gumdrop hat, roll out a large gumdrop on a generously sugared surface. Cut 1 rounded piece to look like the top of the hat and 1 straight piece to look like the brim of the hat as shown in the photo. Overlap the pieces to make the hat: pipe decorator gel over the seam for the hat band.

continued on page 28

26

Scarecrow Cupcakes, continued

Maple Frosting

    2 tablespoons butter, softened
    2 tablespoons maple or pancake syrup
 1 ½ cups powdered sugar

• Beat butter and syrup in medium bowl until blended. Gradually beat in powdered sugar until smooth.   *Makes about 1 ½ cups*

Ice Cream Cone Cupcakes

  1 package (about 18 ounces) white cake mix, plus ingredients
       to prepare mix
  2 tablespoons nonpareils*
24 flat-bottomed ice cream cones
    Prepared vanilla and chocolate frostings
    Additional nonpareils and decors

Nonpareils are tiny, round, brightly colored sprinkles used for cake and cookie decorating.

1. Preheat oven to 350°F.

2. Prepare cake mix according to package directions. Stir in nonpareils.

3. Spoon ¼ cup batter into each ice cream cone.

4. Stand cones in 13×9-inch baking pan or in muffin pan cups. Bake about 20 minutes or until toothpicks inserted into centers come out clean. Cool completely on wire racks.

5. Frost cupcakes and decorate as desired.   *Makes 24 cupcakes*

Note: Cupcakes are best served the day they are prepared. Store loosely covered.

Turkey Cupcakes

  1 package (about 18 ounces) cake mix (any flavor), plus ingredients to prepare mix
  1 container (16 ounces) chocolate frosting
  ¾ cup marshmallow creme
  24 shortbread ring cookies
  2 sticks white spearmint gum
  48 small red candies
    Candy corn and assorted candies for decoration

1. Preheat oven to 350°F. Line 24 standard (2½-inch) muffin pan cups with paper baking cups.

2. Prepare cake mix according to package directions. Spoon batter into prepared muffin cups.

3. Bake 15 to 20 minutes or until toothpicks inserted into centers come out clean. Cool in pans on wire racks 10 minutes. Remove from pans to wire racks; cool completely.

4. Combine frosting and marshmallow creme in medium bowl; mix well. Frost cupcakes lightly with frosting mixture; reserve remaining frosting mixture.

5. Cut cookies in half. Cut 24 halves in half again to form quarters.

6. For each cupcake, stand 1 cookie half upright on back edge of cupcake for tail. Place 1 cookie quarter on opposite side of cupcake for head; discard or reserve remaining cookie quarters for another use. Frost cookies with remaining frosting mixture to blend in with cupcake.

7. Cut gum into ¼-inch pieces; trim both ends of gum into points. Fold gum in half to form beaks; place on bottom edges of heads. Position candies on heads for eyes. Decorate top of tails with candies as desired.

Makes 24 cupcakes

His and Her Cupcakes

1 package (about 18 ounces) cake mix, any flavor, plus
    ingredients to prepare mix
1 container (16 ounces) vanilla frosting
3 rolls (¾ ounce each) fruit leather, cut into 4×2⅜-inch strips
12 pieces striped fruit gum
    Red food coloring
24 vanilla wafer cookies
    Small candies

1. Line 24 standard (2½-inch) muffin pan cups with paper liners or spray with nonstick cooking spray. Prepare cake mix and bake in muffin cups according to package directions. Cool in pans on wire racks 15 minutes. Remove cupcakes to wire racks; cool completely.

2. For "His" cupcakes, frost 12 cupcakes. Place 1 strip fruit leather on each frosted cupcake to form shirt collar. Cut gum into tie shapes and place on cupcakes.

3. For "Her" cupcakes, tint remaining frosting pink with food coloring. Frost remaining cupcakes with tinted frosting. Use dab of frosting to sandwich two vanilla wafers together. Repeat with remaining cookies. Frost cookie sandwiches pink. Top each cupcake with frosted cookie sandwich, placing slightly off-center for crown of hat. Decorate hats with fruit leather and candies.

Makes 24 cupcakes

● ● ● **SUPER SUGGESTION** ● ● ●

**If you don't have muffin pans, don't worry.
Foil baking cups are sturdy enough to be used
without muffin pans; simply place the baking cups
on a baking sheet and fill.**

● ● ● ● ● ● ● ● ● ● ● ● ● ● ●

Double Malted Cupcakes

Cupcakes

　2 cups all-purpose flour
　¼ cup malted milk powder
　2 teaspoons baking powder
　¼ teaspoon salt
　1¾ cups granulated sugar
　½ cup (1 stick) butter, softened
　1 cup 2% or whole milk
　1½ teaspoons vanilla
　3 egg whites

Frosting

　4 ounces milk chocolate candy bar, broken into chunks
　¼ cup (½ stick) butter
　¼ cup whipping cream
　1 tablespoon malted milk powder
　1 teaspoon vanilla
　1¾ cups powdered sugar
　30 chocolate-covered malt ball candies

1. Preheat oven to 350°F. Line 30 standard (2½-inch) muffin pan cups with paper baking cups.

2. For cupcakes, combine flour, ¼ cup malted milk powder, baking powder and salt; mix well and set aside. Beat sugar and ½ cup butter with electric mixer at medium speed 1 minute. Add milk and 1½ teaspoons vanilla. Beat at low speed 30 seconds. Gradually beat in flour mixture; beat at medium speed 2 minutes. Add egg whites; beat 1 minute.

3. Spoon batter into prepared muffin cups filling ⅔ full. Bake 20 minutes or until golden brown and toothpicks inserted into centers come out clean. Cool in pans on wire racks 10 minutes. (Centers of cupcakes will sink slightly upon cooling.) Remove cupcakes to racks; cool completely. (At this point, cupcakes may be frozen up to 3 months.)

4. For frosting, melt chocolate and ¼ cup butter in heavy medium saucepan over low heat, stirring frequently. Stir in cream, 1 tablespoon malted milk powder and 1 teaspoon vanilla; mix well. Gradually stir in powdered sugar. Cook 4 to 5 minutes, stirring constantly, until small lumps disappear. Remove from heat. Refrigerate 20 minutes, beating every 5 minutes or until frosting is spreadable.

5. Spread cooled cupcakes with frosting; decorate with chocolate-covered malt ball candies. Store at room temperature up to 24 hours or cover and refrigerate for up to 3 days before serving.   *Makes 30 cupcakes*

Cream Filled Cupcakes

    1 package (8 ounces) cream cheese, softened
    ½ cup powdered sugar
    ⅓ cup thawed frozen limeade concentrate
    1 teaspoon vanilla
       Yellow and blue food coloring
    1 package (about 18 ounces) chocolate cake mix
    1 egg
       Water and vegetable oil
    1 container (16 ounces) vanilla frosting
       Orange sugar

1. Preheat oven to 350°F. Line 24 standard (2½-inch) muffin pan cups with paper baking liners, or spray with nonstick cooking spray.

2. Combine cream cheese, powdered sugar, limeade concentrate and vanilla in large bowl. Beat with electric mixer at medium speed until well blended. Tint with yellow food coloring; beat until well blended. Set aside.

3. Prepare cake mix according to package directions using 1 egg, water and oil. Spoon batter into prepared muffin cups, filling half full. Spoon 1 rounded teaspoon cream cheese mixture in center of each cup.

4. Bake about 20 minutes or until toothpicks inserted into centers come out clean. Cool completely on wire racks.

5. Add 4 drops yellow food coloring and 2 drops blue food coloring to frosting. Stir until well blended; adjust color as needed by adding additional food coloring 1 drop at a time, blending well after each addition. Spread frosting on cooled cupcakes. Sprinkle with sugar.   *Makes 24 cupcakes*

Reindeer Cupcakes

1 package (about 18 ounces) chocolate cake mix, plus ingredients
   to prepare mix
¼ cup (½ stick) butter, softened
4 cups powdered sugar
5 to 6 tablespoons brewed espresso
½ cup (3 ounces) semisweet chocolate chips, melted
1 teaspoon vanilla
   Dash salt
24 pretzel twists, broken in half
   Assorted candies for decoration

1. Preheat oven to 350°F. Line 24 standard (2½-inch) muffin pan cups with paper baking cups.

2. Prepare cake mix according to package directions. Spoon batter into prepared muffin cups. Bake 15 to 20 minutes or until toothpicks inserted into centers come out clean. Cool in pans on wire racks 10 minutes. Remove cupcakes to racks; cool completely.

3. Beat butter in large bowl with electric mixer at medium speed until creamy. Gradually add powdered sugar and 4 tablespoons espresso; beat until smooth. Add melted chocolate, vanilla and salt; beat until well blended. Add remaining espresso, 1 tablespoon at a time, until frosting is of desired spreading consistency.

4. Frost cooled cupcakes with frosting. Decorate with broken pretzel pieces for antlers and assorted candies for reindeer faces.

Makes 24 cupcakes

Magical Wizard Hats

1 package (about 18 ounces) cake mix (any flavor), plus
    ingredients to prepare mix
2 containers (16 ounces each) vanilla frosting
    Yellow and purple or black food colorings
2 packages (4 ounces each) sugar cones
    Orange sugar, decors and black decorating gel

1. Line 24 standard (2½-inch) muffin pan cups with paper baking liners, or spray with nonstick cooking spray. Prepare cake mix and bake in muffin cups according to package directions. Cool in pans on wire racks 15 minutes. Remove cupcakes from pan; cool completely on wire racks.

2. Frost cupcakes. Place ½ cup remaining frosting in small bowl; tint with yellow food coloring. Tint remaining frosting with purple or black food coloring.

3. Spread sugar cones with dark frosting, covering completely. Place 1 cone upside down on each frosted cupcake. Spoon yellow frosting into small resealable plastic food storage bag. Cut off small corner of bag. Pipe yellow frosting around base of each frosted cone. Decorate as desired.

Makes 24 cupcakes

● ● ● ● SUPER SUGGESTION ● ● ● ●

To easily fill muffin cups, place batter in a 4-cup glass measure. Use a plastic spatula to control the flow of the batter.

● ● ● ● ● ● ● ● ● ● ● ● ●

Spider Cupcakes

1 package (about 18 ounces) yellow or white cake mix
1 cup solid-pack pumpkin
¾ cup water
3 eggs
2 tablespoons vegetable oil
1 teaspoon ground cinnamon
1 teaspoon pumpkin pie spice*
  Orange food coloring
1 container (16 ounces) vanilla, cream cheese or caramel
    frosting
4 ounces semisweet chocolate
4 dozen black gumdrops

Substitute ½ teaspoon ground cinnamon, ¼ teaspoon ground ginger and ⅛ teaspoon each ground allspice and ground nutmeg for 1 teaspoon pumpkin pie spice.

1. Preheat oven to 350°F. Line 24 standard (2½-inch) muffin pan cups with paper baking liners, or spray with nonstick cooking spray.

2. Combine cake mix, pumpkin, water, eggs, oil, cinnamon and pumpkin pie spice in large bowl. Beat at medium speed of electric mixer 3 minutes or until well blended.

3. Spoon ¼ cup batter into each muffin cup. Bake about 20 minutes or until toothpicks inserted into centers come out clean. Cool 10 minutes on wire rack. Remove cupcakes from pan; cool completely.

4. Add orange food coloring to frosting. Stir until well blended; adjust color as needed by adding additional food coloring 1 drop at a time, blending well after each addition. Frost cupcakes.

5. Place chocolate in small resealable plastic food storage bag. Microwave at MEDIUM (50% power) 40 seconds. Knead bag; microwave 30 seconds to 1 minute or until chocolate is melted. Knead bag until chocolate is smooth. Cut off tiny corner of bag. Drizzle chocolate in four or five concentric circles over top of one cupcake. Immediately draw 6 to 8 lines at regular intervals from center to edges of cupcake with toothpick or knife to make web. Repeat with remaining cupcakes and chocolate.

6. For spider, place one gumdrop in center of web design on top of cupcake. Roll out another gumdrop with rolling pin. Slice thinly and roll into "legs." Place legs onto cupcake to complete spider. Repeat with remaining gumdrops and cupcakes. *Makes 24 to 27 cupcakes*

Spider Cupcakes

Candy Corn by the Slice

1 package (10 ounces) refrigerated pizza crust dough
2 cups (8 ounces) shredded Cheddar cheese, divided
2 tablespoons paprika
¼ cup white cheese sauce*
½ cup shredded mozzarella cheese
⅓ cup tomato sauce

*To make a white cheese sauce, mix 3 tablespoons vegetable broth with 3 tablespoons mascarpone cheese in a small saucepan over low heat, until melted. Season with salt and white pepper to taste.

1. Preheat oven to 400°F. Spray 13-inch round pizza pan with cooking spray. Fit pizza dough into pan, shaping as needed.

2. Place 1 cup Cheddar cheese in medium bowl. Add paprika and stir until cheese is evenly colored; set aside. Make white cheese sauce.

3. Spread white cheese sauce in center of pizza in 4-inch diameter circle. Arrange mozzarella cheese on top of white sauce. Place 3-inch ring of tomato sauce around center circle; top with paprika and Cheddar cheese mixture. Use remaining 1 cup Cheddar cheese to create 1½-inch border around edge of pizza.

4. Bake 12 to 15 minutes or until edge is lightly browned and cheese is melted and bubbling. Cut into wedges to serve.   *Makes 8 slices*

Mice Creams

1 pint vanilla ice cream
1 (4-ounce) package READY CRUST® Mini-Graham Cracker Pie Crusts
Ears—12 KEEBLER® Grasshopper® cookies
Tails—3 chocolate twigs, broken in half *or* 6 (3-inch) pieces black shoestring licorice
Eyes and noses—18 brown candy-coated chocolate candies
Whiskers—2 teaspoons chocolate sprinkles

1. Place 1 scoop vanilla ice cream into each crust. Press cookie ears and tails into ice cream. Press eyes, noses and whiskers in place. Serve immediately. Do not refreeze.   *Makes 6 servings*

Ghosts at the Watering Hole

    1 package (12 ounces) chocolate chips
    ½ cup whipping cream
    2 tablespoons light corn syrup
    1 tablespoon butter
      Pinch salt
      Marshmallows

1. Combine chips, cream, corn syrup, butter and salt in small saucepan. Heat over low heat until chips melt and mixture is smooth. Pour into fondue pot; set over low heat.

2. Place marshmallows in serving bowl. Set out stack of dessert plates and fondue forks for dipping.   *Makes about 2 cups (12 servings)*

Bewitching Cocoa Bites

    5 cups crisp rice cereal
    6 tablespoons butter or margarine
    3 cups miniature marshmallows or 30 large marshmallows
  1⅔ cups (10-ounce package) REESE'S® Peanut Butter Chips
    ⅓ cup HERSHEY®S Cocoa
    ⅓ cup light corn syrup

1. Measure cereal; set aside. Melt butter in large saucepan over low heat. Add marshmallows, peanut butter chips and cocoa. Cook over low heat, stirring constantly, until marshmallows and chips are melted. Remove from heat. Stir in corn syrup. Add cereal; stir until well coated.

2. Shape mixture into 1½-inch balls, stirring a few times during shaping. Place on cookie sheet. Cool completely. Store in cool dry place.
                                        Makes about 3½ dozen treats

Microwave Directions: Microwave butter covered in large microwave-safe bowl at HIGH (100%) 45 seconds or until melted. Add marshmallows, peanut butter chips and cocoa; stir. Microwave at HIGH 1½ minutes; stir until mixture is smooth. Stir in corn syrup. Add cereal; stir until well coated. Shape as directed above.

50

Brrrrownie Cats

    1 cup (2 sticks) unsalted butter
    4 ounces unsweetened chocolate
 1½ cups sugar
    3 eggs
    1 cup all-purpose flour
 ¼ teaspoon salt
    Black frosting, jimmies and other decorations as desired

1. Preheat oven to 350°F. Grease 13×9-inch baking pan. Melt butter and chocolate in small microwavable bowl on HIGH 1 to 1½ minutes.

2. Transfer butter mixture to large bowl. Stir in sugar until well blended. Beat in eggs, one at a time. Stir in flour and salt.

3. Spread batter into prepared pan. Bake 20 to 25 minutes or just until firm. Cool completely on wire rack. Using cookie cutters, cut brownies into cat shapes. Decorate as desired.   *Makes about 2 dozen brownies*

Cauldron Dipped Apples

    8 to 10 medium apples, stems removed
    8 to 10 wooden ice cream sticks
    Peanut Butter Sugar (page 54)
    2 cups (12-ounce package) HERSHEY₁S Semi-Sweet Chocolate Chips
 ¼ cup shortening (do *not* use butter, margarine, spread or oil)
 ⅔ cup REESE'S® Creamy Peanut Butter
 ⅔ cup powdered sugar

1. Line tray with wax paper. Wash and dry apples; insert wooden stick into stem end of each apple. Prepare Peanut Butter Sugar.

2. Melt chocolate chips and shortening in medium saucepan over low heat. Remove from heat. Add peanut butter; stir until melted and smooth. With whisk, blend in powdered sugar.

3. Dip apples into chocolate mixture; twirl gently to remove excess. Sprinkle Peanut Butter Sugar over apples. Place on prepared tray. Refrigerate until coating is firm. Store in refrigerator.   *Makes 8 to 10 dipped apples*

continued on page 54

Brrrrownie Cats, Sugar & Spice Jack-O'-Lantern Cookies (page 54)

Cauldron Dipped Apples, continued

Peanut Butter Sugar

3 tablespoons REESE'S® Creamy or Crunchy Peanut Butter
⅓ cup powdered sugar
1 tablespoon granulated sugar

Combine all ingredients in small bowl.   *Makes about ⅔ cup*

Sugar & Spice Jack-O'-Lantern Cookies

2⅓ cups all-purpose flour
2 teaspoons ground cinnamon
1½ teaspoons *each* baking powder and ground ginger
½ teaspoon salt
¼ teaspoon nutmeg
¾ cup (1½ sticks) butter, softened
½ cup packed brown sugar
½ cup molasses
1 egg
Orange frosting, jimmies and other decorations as desired

1. Combine flour, cinnamon, baking powder, ginger, salt and nutmeg in medium bowl. Beat butter and sugar in large bowl at medium speed of electric mixer until light and fluffy. Add molasses and egg; beat until well blended. Gradually beat in flour mixture until just combined.

2. Form dough into 2 balls; press into 2-inch-thick discs. Wrap in plastic wrap; refrigerate at least 1 hour or until firm. Let stand at room temperature to soften slightly.

3. Preheat oven to 350°F. Roll out dough on lightly floured surface to ¼-inch thickness. Cut out cookies with jack-o'-lantern cookie cutters. Place cutouts on *ungreased* cookie sheets. Bake about 12 to 14 minutes or until centers are firm. Let cookies stand on cookie sheets 1 minute; cool completely on wire racks. Frost and decorate as desired.

Makes 2 to 3 dozen cookies

Jack-O-Lantern Bars

Bars
> 2 cups all-purpose flour
> 2 cups DOMINO® Granulated Sugar
> 2 teaspoons *each* baking powder and pumpkin pie spice
> 1 teaspoon baking soda
> ½ teaspoon salt
> 4 eggs, beaten
> 1 (15-ounce) can pumpkin (about 2 cups)
> 1 cup oil

Frosting
> 2 cups DOMINO® Confectioners Sugar
> 1 (3-ounce) package cream cheese, softened
> ⅓ cup butter or margarine, softened
> 1 tablespoon milk
> 1 teaspoon vanilla
> 3 drops yellow food color
> 2 drops red food color

Decorations
> Fall color candy corn and melted chocolate

Heat oven to 350°F. Grease and flour 15×10×1-inch baking pan. Combine all dry ingredients for bars in large bowl; mix well. Add eggs, pumpkin and oil. Stir until well blended. Pour into pan. Bake for 25 to 30 minutes or until toothpick inserted in center comes out clean. Cool completely.

Mix frosting ingredients in small bowl until smooth. Frost cooled bars. Cut into squares. Decorate as desired.   *Makes 24 bars*

Quick Melted Chocolate for Piping: Place ¼ cup chocolate chips in small resealable plastic bag. Seal. Place in bowl of very warm water, being careful to keep interior of bag dry. Knead chocolate occasionally until melted. Dry bag thoroughly. Cut small opening in tip of bag. Squeeze chocolate out to pipe on decorations. Chocolate can also be melted in plastic bag in microwave oven. Microwave on MEDIUM for 30 seconds at a time, checking and kneading chocolate until melted.

Preparation Time: 20 minutes
Baking Time: 30 minutes
Cooling Time: 1½ hours
Frost and Decorate Time: 20 minutes

Monster Sandwiches

    8 assorted round and oblong sandwich rolls
      Butter
   16 to 24 slices assorted cold cuts (salami, turkey, ham and/or
      bologna)
    6 to 8 slices assorted cheeses (American, Swiss and/or
      Muenster)
    1 firm tomato, sliced
    1 cucumber, sliced thinly
      Assorted lettuce leaves (Romaine, curly and/or red leaf)
      Cocktail onions, green and black olives, cherry tomatoes,
      pickled gherkins, radishes, baby corn and/or hard-boiled
      eggs

1. Cut rolls open just below center; spread with butter.

2. Layer meats, cheeses, tomato, cucumber and greens to make monster faces. Roll "tongues" from ham slices or make "lips" with tomato slices.

3. Use toothpicks to affix remaining ingredients for eyes, ears, fins, horns and hair as desired.   *Makes 8 sandwiches*

Note: Remember to remove toothpicks before eating.

Ghost on a Stick

    4 wooden craft sticks
    4 medium pears, stems removed
    9 squares (2 ounces each) almond bark
      Mini chocolate chips

1. Line baking sheet with waxed paper and 4 paper baking cups. Insert wooden sticks into stem ends of pears.

2. Melt almond bark according to package directions.

3. Dip one pear into melted almond bark, spooning bark over top to coat evenly. Remove excess by scraping pear bottom across rim of measuring cup. Place on paper baking cup; let set 1 minute.

4. Decorate with mini chocolate chips to make ghost face. Repeat with remaining pears. Place spoonful of extra almond bark at bottom of pears for ghost tails. Refrigerate until firm.   *Makes 4 servings*

Frightful Finger Cookies

I cup (2 sticks) unsalted butter
¾ cup powdered sugar
I teaspoon vanilla
½ teaspoon salt
I¾ cups all-purpose flour
I cup ground pecans
Red food coloring and blanched or slivered almonds
(optional)

1. Preheat oven to 300°F. Line cookie sheets with parchment paper.

2. Beat butter and sugar in bowl of electric mixer until light and fluffy. Add vanilla and salt. Add flour, ¼ cup at a time, blending well after each addition. Stir in pecans. Dough will be heavy.

3. Using I heaping tablespoonful per cookie, shape dough into "fingers" about 3 inches long and ¾ inch in diameter.

4. Place dough on prepared cookie sheets. Using a knife, lightly score "fingers" a few times across center and near top to resemble knuckles. "Paint" almonds with food coloring and press into top of each cookie to resemble "fingernail", if desired. Or, make an indentation in cookie top to resemble "fingernail".

5. Bake 25 minutes or until lightly brown. Cool I minute on cookie sheets. Remove to wire racks; cool completely.   *Makes about 3 dozen cookies*

● ● ● ● SUPER SUGGESTION ● ● ● ●

Shiny, heavy-gauge aluminum baking sheets promote
even browning of cookies; dark pans absorb more
heat causing cookies to brown too quickly. When using
dark sheets, reduce oven temperature by 25°F.

● ● ● ● ● ● ● ● ● ● ● ● ● ●

Cowboy in a Shroud

1 pound boneless skinless chicken thighs or breasts
1 cup chicken broth
1 can (14½ ounces) diced tomatoes
2 cans (11 ounces each) condensed nacho cheese soup, undiluted
1 can (4 ounces) diced green chiles, drained
6 flour tortillas (8-inch diameter)
1 cup Mexican cheese blend
4 roasted red peppers
   Capers, peppercorns and minced fresh cilantro for garnish

1. Preheat oven to 350°F. Place chicken in small saucepan with broth. Cover; cook over low heat 20 minutes or until chicken reaches internal temperature of 180°F. Remove from heat and reserve broth. Cut chicken into bite-size strips. Set aside.

2. Combine tomatoes, nacho cheese soup and chiles in bowl. Divide nacho cheese soup mixture in half. Add chicken to one half and ½ cup reserved chicken broth to other half.

3. Spoon chicken mixture down center of each flour tortilla; roll up. Tortillas will be very full.

4. Pour half of nacho-chicken broth mixture into 9- to 10-inch square glass baking dish. Arrange filled tortillas seam-side down in baking dish, packing tightly. Spoon on remaining nacho-chicken broth mixture. Sprinkle with cheese. Bake 20 to 25 minutes or until filling is hot and cheese is melted.

5. Garnish with slice of roasted red pepper, cut into 3-inch triangle for "bandana." Make cowboy face with capers, peppercorns or cilantro.

Makes 6 main dish or 12 appetizer servings

Yolkensteins

8 hard-cooked eggs
8 small tomato slices
8 toothpicks
  Mayonnaise
8 pimiento-stuffed olives
8 black peppercorns
  Parsley
16 whole cloves

1. Cut thin slice from wide end of egg so it stands upright.

2. Slice egg horizontally, about $\frac{1}{3}$ up from bottom.

3. Place tomato slice on bottom piece of egg. Insert toothpick upright in middle of tomato slice and egg for "spine." Reattach top piece of egg.

4. Using dabs of mayonnaise, attach slices of olives for "eyes" and peppercorn for "nose." Attach parsley for hair and stick 1 whole clove on each side of egg under tomato slice for "bolts."

5. Pipe mayonnaise "teeth" on tomato slice just before serving. Repeat for all eggs.

Makes 8 servings

● ● ● **SUPER SUGGESTION** ● ● ●

Try serving these frightfully good treats to your kids for Halloween breakfast! Put out tiny plates of seasoned salt, sesame seeds, grated cheese and celery salt for dipping the eggs.

● ● ● ● ● ● ● ● ● ● ● ● ● ●

Green Meanies

 4 green apples
 1 cup nut butter (cashew, almond or peanut butter)
 Almond slivers

1. Place apple, stem side up, on cutting board. Cut away 2 halves from sides of apple, leaving 1-inch-thick center slice with stem and core. Discard core slice. Cut each half round into 4 wedges using crinkle cutter. Repeat with remaining apples. Each apple will yield 8 wedges.

2. Spread 2 teaspoons nut butter on wide edge of apple slice. Top with another crinkled edge apple slice, aligning crinkled edges to resemble jaws. Insert almond slivers to make fangs. *Makes 8 servings*

Tip: For best effect, use a crinkle cutter garnishing tool to create a toothy look.

Black Cat Fudge

 8 ounces semisweet chocolate, coarsely chopped
 1/4 cup butter
 1/3 cup light corn syrup
 1/4 cup whipping cream
 1 teaspoon vanilla
 1/4 teaspoon salt
 4 1/2 cups (16 ounces) powdered sugar, sifted
 White chocolate chips (about 30)

1. Line 11×7-inch pan with foil, extending foil beyond edges of pan; grease foil.

2. Melt chocolate and butter in medium saucepan over low heat; stir in corn syrup, cream, vanilla and salt. Remove from heat and gradually stir in powdered sugar until smooth.

3. Spread evenly in prepared pan. Refrigerate until firm, 1 to 2 hours.

4. Using foil as handles, remove fudge from pan; peel off foil. Cut into squares or use cookie cutters to cut out cats. Frequently clean knife with warm water and dry thoroughly to prevent sticking. Place 2 vanilla milk chips on each cat for eyes. Score feet to make claws. Cover; refrigerate until ready to serve. *Makes about 1 1/2 pounds (12 to 15 cats)*

Caterpillar Chicken with Mushroom Ooze

I package (about 17 ounces) frozen puff pastry sheets, thawed
   according to package directions
I tablespoon vegetable oil
I cup minced celery
½ cup minced onion
I can (10¾ ounces) cream of mushroom soup
¾ cup milk
¼ teaspoon garlic salt
⅛ teaspoon white pepper
2 cups chopped cooked chicken breast
   Fresh chives and/or black olives for decorating (optional)

1. Preheat oven to 400°F. Using round cookie cutter, cut each pastry sheet section into 4 to 5 rounds. Place rounds on ungreased cookie sheet, overlapping each round to create caterpillar. Repeat with additional rounds for total of 6 caterpillars. Bake 17 to 20 minutes or until golden. Remove from baking sheet and cool on wire rack. Use knife to remove top of circles and hollow out soft pastry underneath to make "shell."

2. Heat oil in skillet over medium heat. Add celery and onion; cook until tender. Add soup, milk, salt and pepper. Bring to a boil; reduce heat to low. Simmer, covered, 5 minutes. Add chicken; heat through. Spoon chicken mixture into puff pastry shells. Decorate with fresh chives and black olives, if desired.   *Makes 6 servings*

● ● ● SUPER SUGGESTION ● ● ●

Thoroughly wash cutting surfaces, utensils and
your hands with hot soapy water after coming
in contact with uncooked chicken. This eliminates
the risk of contaminating other foods with salmonella
bacteria that is often present in raw chicken.
Salmonella is killed during cooking.

● ● ● ● ● ● ● ● ● ● ● ● ● ●

Wormy Apples

6 medium apples, such as Jonathan or Pink Lady
½ cup maple syrup
⅓ cup water
1 teaspoon lemon juice
2 (1-inch) strips lemon peel
¼ teaspoon ground cinnamon
  Dash salt
2 tablespoons butter
6 to 12 soft candy worms

1. Preheat oven to 350°F. Core apples and peel top ⅓ of apple. Stand apples in baking pan.

2. Combine maple syrup, water, lemon juice, lemon peel, cinnamon and salt in small saucepan. Bring to a boil. Pour mixture over apples. Cover loosely with foil.

3. Bake 30 minutes. Remove from oven. Place 1 teaspoon butter into core of each apple. Baste apples with pan juices; cover and bake 15 minutes or until tender. Cool.

4. Cut 1 or 2 small holes from outside of apple through to core. Thread worms halfway through holes. Serve warm or cold.   *Makes 6 servings*

Black Cat Cookies

1 package (18 ounces) refrigerated sugar cookie dough
All-purpose flour (optional)
White Decorator Icing (recipe follows)
Black paste food coloring
Assorted colored candies

1. Preheat oven to 350°F. Remove dough from wrapper according to package directions. Divide dough in half. Reserve 1 half; cover and refrigerate remaining half.

2. Roll reserved dough on lightly floured surface to $\frac{1}{8}$-inch thickness. Sprinkle with flour to minimize sticking, if necessary.

3. Cut out dough using 3$\frac{1}{2}$-inch cat face cookie cutter. Place cutouts 2 inches apart on ungreased baking sheets. Repeat with remaining dough and scraps.

4. Bake 8 to 10 minutes or until firm but not browned. Cool on baking sheets 2 minutes. Remove to wire racks; cool completely.

5. Prepare White Decorator Icing. Add desired amount of food coloring to make black. Decorate cookies with icing and assorted candies as desired to make cat faces. *Makes about 20 cookies*

White Decorator Icing

4 cups powdered sugar
$\frac{1}{2}$ cup shortening or unsalted butter
1 tablespoon corn syrup
6 to 8 tablespoons milk

Beat all ingredients in medium bowl 2 minutes or until fluffy.

Parmesan Ranch Snack Mix

3 cups bite-size corn or rice cereal

2 cups oyster crackers

1 package (5 ounces) bagel chips, broken in half

1½ cups pretzel twists

1 cup pistachios

2 tablespoons grated Parmesan cheese

¼ cup butter, melted

1 package (1 ounce) dry ranch salad dressing mix

½ teaspoon garlic powder

Slow Cooker Directions

1. Combine cereal, oyster crackers, bagel chips, pretzels, pistachios and Parmesan cheese in slow cooker; mix gently.

2. Combine butter, salad dressing mix and garlic powder in small bowl. Pour over cereal mixture; toss lightly to coat. Cover; cook on LOW 3 hours.

3. Remove cover and stir gently. Continue to cook, uncovered, on LOW 30 minutes.

Makes about 9½ cups snack mix

Prep Time: 5 minutes
Cook Time: 3½ hours

Celtic Knots

1 package (16 ounces) hot roll mix plus ingredients to prepare mix
1 egg white
2 teaspoons water
2 tablespoons coarse salt

1. Prepare hot roll mix according to package directions.

2. Preheat oven to 375°F. Lightly grease baking sheets; set aside.

3. Divide dough equally into 16 pieces; shape each piece into 10-inch rope. Form each rope into interlocking ring as shown in photo; place on prepared baking sheets. Moisten ends of rope at seams; pinch to seal.

4. Beat egg white and water in small bowl until foamy. Brush onto dough shapes; sprinkle with coarse salt.

5. Bake about 15 minutes or until golden brown. Serve warm or at room temperature.

Makes 16 knots

Leapin' Lizards!

1 cup butterscotch-flavor chips
½ cup corn syrup
3 tablespoons butter
1 cup white chocolate chips
Green food coloring
7 cups crisp rice cereal
Candy corn, green jelly beans, red miniature jaw breakers and chocolate chips

1. Line baking sheet with waxed paper.

2. Combine butterscotch chips, corn syrup and butter in large saucepan. Stir over medium heat until chips are melted. Add white chocolate chips and green food coloring; stir well. Remove from heat. Add cereal; stir to coat evenly.

3. Lightly butter hands and shape about 1½ cups cereal mixture into lizard (about 6 inches long). Place on prepared baking sheet. Decorate with candies. Repeat with remaining mixture.

Makes 4 lizards

Dino-Mite Dinosaurs

    1 cup (2 sticks) butter, softened
1¼ cups granulated sugar
    1 large egg
    2 squares (1 ounce each) semi-sweet chocolate, melted
½ teaspoon vanilla extract
2⅓ cups all-purpose flour
    1 teaspoon baking powder
¼ teaspoon salt
    1 cup white frosting
    Assorted food colorings
    1 cup "M&M's"® Chocolate Mini Baking Bits

In large bowl cream butter and sugar until light and fluffy; beat in egg, chocolate and vanilla. In medium bowl combine flour, baking powder and salt; add to creamed mixture. Wrap and refrigerate dough 2 to 3 hours. Preheat oven to 350°F. Working with half the dough at a time on lightly floured surface, roll to ¼-inch thickness. Cut into dinosaur shapes using 4-inch cookie cutters. Place about 2 inches apart on ungreased cookie sheets. Bake 10 to 12 minutes. Cool 2 minutes on cookie sheets; cool completely on wire racks. Tint frosting to desired colors. Frost cookies and decorate with "M&M's"® Chocolate Mini Baking Bits. Store in tightly covered container.   *Makes 2 dozen cookies*

Pasta Snacks

4 ounces uncooked pasta (wagon wheels, bowties or cork screws)
Vegetable oil for deep frying
2 tablespoons grated Parmesan cheese
1 tablespoon ground walnuts
1/8 teaspoon garlic salt

Cook pasta according to package directions; drain. Rinse in cold water and drain well. Spread cooked pasta on paper towels to remove additional water.

Heat 2 inches oil in deep fat fryer or deep saucepan to 400°F. Fry pasta, a few at a time, until golden, about 30 to 45 seconds. Remove with slotted spoon; drain thoroughly. Mix cheese, walnuts and garlic salt; toss with fried pasta. Store in airtight container. *Makes 2½ cups*

Favorite recipe from **North Dakota Wheat Commission**

"Here's Looking at You" Yummies

½ cup creamy or crunchy peanut butter
2 tablespoons butter, softened
¾ to 1 cup powdered sugar, divided
1¼ cups crisp rice cereal
1¼ cups "M&M's"® Semi-Sweet Chocolate Mini Baking Bits, divided
4 squares (2 ounces each) almond bark
Red decorating gel

Line cookie sheet with waxed paper; set aside. In large bowl combine peanut butter and butter. Stir in ½ cup powdered sugar until well blended. Stir in cereal and 1 cup "M&M's"® Semi-Sweet Chocolate Mini Baking Bits. Stir in ¼ cup powdered sugar. If mixture is too sticky, stir in remaining ¼ cup powdered sugar. Shape dough into 1½-inch balls. Place on prepared cookie sheet. Refrigerate 1 hour. Line another cookie sheet with waxed paper; set aside. Melt almond bark according to package directions. Dip one ball into almond bark; gently shake off excess. Place treat on prepared cookie sheet. Decorate with remaining ¼ cup "M&M's"® Semi-Sweet Chocolate Mini Baking Bits and decorating gel to look like eyes. Store in tightly covered container. *Makes 2 dozen treats*

Magic Wands

    1 cup semisweet chocolate chips
  12 pretzel rods
    3 ounces white chocolate baking bars or confectionery coating
      Red and yellow food colorings
      Assorted sprinkles
      Ribbon

1. Line baking sheet with waxed paper.

2. Melt semisweet chocolate in top of double boiler over hot, not boiling, water. Remove from heat. Dip pretzel rods into chocolate, spooning chocolate to coat about ¾ of each pretzel. Place on prepared baking sheet. Refrigerate until chocolate is firm.

3. Melt white chocolate in top of clean double boiler over hot, not boiling, water. Stir in food colorings to make orange. Remove from heat. Dip coated pretzels quickly into colored white chocolate to coat about ¼ of each pretzel.

4. Place on baking sheet. Immediately top with sprinkles. Refrigerate until chocolate is firm.

5. Tie ends with ribbons.   *Makes 12 wands*

Fun Fruit Kabobs

    4 small strawberries (or 2 large strawberries sliced in half
        lengthwise) with green leaves removed
    4 banana slices (¼ small 4-ounce banana)
    4 green grapes
    4 (2¼-inch) pretzel sticks

1. Gently push 1 strawberry, 1 banana slice and 1 grape onto each pretzel stick. Twist pretzel as you are pushing fruit onto it to keep the pretzel from breaking.

2. Eat right away to keep the pretzels crunchy.   *Makes 1 serving*

Domino Cookies

 I package (20 ounces) refrigerated sugar cookie dough
     All-purpose flour (optional)
 ½ cup semisweet chocolate chips

1. Preheat oven to 350°F. Grease cookie sheets.

2. Remove dough from wrapper according to package directions. Cut dough into 4 equal sections. Reserve 1 section; refrigerate remaining 3 sections.

3. Roll reserved dough to ⅛-inch thickness. Sprinkle with flour to minimize sticking, if necessary. Cut out 9 (2½×1¾-inch) rectangles using sharp knife. Place 2 inches apart on prepared cookie sheets.

4. Score each cookie across middle with sharp knife. Gently press chocolate chips, point side down, into dough to resemble various dominos. Repeat with remaining dough, scraps and chocolate chips.

5. Bake 8 to 10 minutes or until edges are light golden brown. Remove to wire racks; cool completely.   *Makes 3 dozen cookies*

● ● ● SUPER SUGGESTION ● ● ●

**Use these adorable cookies as a learning tool for kids.
They can count the number of chocolate chips in each
cookie and arrange them in lots of ways: highest to lowest,
numerically or even to solve simple math problems. As
a treat, they can eat the cookies afterwards.**

● ● ● ● ● ● ● ● ● ● ● ● ●

Sloppy Joe's Bun Buggies

    4 hot dog buns (not split)
   16 thin slices cucumber or zucchini
   24 thin strips julienned carrots, 1 inch long
    4 ripe olives or pimiento-stuffed olives
      Nonstick cooking spray
    1 (10-ounce) package extra-lean ground turkey
 1 1/4 cups prepared spaghetti sauce
  1/2 cup chopped broccoli stems
    2 teaspoons prepared mustard
  1/2 teaspoon Worcestershire sauce
      Dash salt
      Dash black pepper
    4 small pretzel twists

1. Hollow out hot dog buns. Use toothpick to make four holes in sides of each bun to attach "wheels." Use toothpick to make one hole in center of each cucumber slice; push carrot strip through hole. Press into holes in buns, making "wheels" on buns.

2. Cut each olive in half horizontally. Use toothpick to make two holes in one end of each bun to attach "headlights." Use carrot strips to attach olives to buns, making "headlights."

3. Spray large nonstick skillet with cooking spray. Cook turkey in skillet over medium heat until no longer pink. Stir in spaghetti sauce, broccoli stems, mustard, Worcestershire, salt and pepper; heat through.

4. Spoon sauce mixture into hollowed-out buns. Press pretzel twist into ground turkey mixture, making "windshield" on each buggy.

Makes 4 servings

Sloppy Joe's Bun Buggy

Monster Finger Sandwiches

   1 can (11 ounces) refrigerated breadstick dough
      (12 breadsticks)
   Mustard
12 slices deli ham, cut into ½-inch strips
   4 slices Monterey Jack cheese, cut into ½-inch strips
   1 egg yolk, lightly beaten
   Assorted food colorings

1. Preheat oven to 350°F. Place 6 breadsticks on ungreased baking sheets. Spread with mustard as desired. Divide ham strips evenly among breadsticks, placing over mustard. Repeat with cheese. Top with remaining 6 breadsticks. Gently stretch top dough over filling; press doughs together to seal.

2. Score knuckle and nail lines into each sandwich using sharp knife. Do not cut completely through dough. Tint egg yolk with food coloring as desired. Paint nail with egg yolk mixture.

3. Bake on lower oven rack 12 to 13 minutes or just until light golden. Let cool slightly. Serve warm or cool completely.   *Makes 6 servings*

Caramel Corn

   ½ cup packed brown sugar
   ⅓ cup light corn syrup
   ¼ cup Butter Flavor CRISCO® All-Vegetable Shortening or
      ¼ Butter Flavor CRISCO® Stick
   ½ teaspoon vanilla
   2 quarts popped popcorn
   1 cup coarsely chopped blanched almonds (optional)

Preheat oven to 300°F. Generously grease baking sheet.

In Dutch oven blend brown sugar, corn syrup, Butter Flavor CRISCO® and vanilla. Cook over medium-high heat for about 2 minutes, or until light and foamy, stirring constantly. Remove from heat. Add popcorn, tossing to coat. Stir in almonds. Spread on prepared baking sheet.

Bake at 300°F for 15 minutes, stirring once. Cool. Break into bite-size pieces. Store in covered container.   *Makes 8 cups*

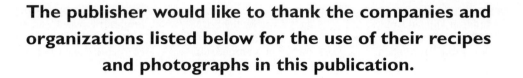

The publisher would like to thank the companies and organizations listed below for the use of their recipes and photographs in this publication.

ACH FOOD COMPANIES, INC.

Dole Food Company, Inc.

Domino® Foods, Inc.

Eagle Brand® Sweetened Condensed Milk

Florida's Citrus Growers

Hershey Foods Corporation

Keebler® Company

© Mars, Incorporated 2005

Mott's® is a registered trademark of Mott's, LLP

North Dakota Wheat Commission

Crisco is a registered trademark of the J.M. Smucker Company

The Sugar Association, Inc.

Sun•Maid® Growers of California

Reprinted with permission of Sunkist Growers, Inc.

Wheat Foods Council

Index

METRIC CONVERSION CHART

VOLUME MEASUREMENTS (dry)

$\frac{1}{8}$ teaspoon = 0.5 mL
$\frac{1}{4}$ teaspoon = 1 mL
$\frac{1}{2}$ teaspoon = 2 mL
$\frac{3}{4}$ teaspoon = 4 mL
1 teaspoon = 5 mL
1 tablespoon = 15 mL
2 tablespoons = 30 mL
$\frac{1}{4}$ cup = 60 mL
$\frac{1}{3}$ cup = 75 mL
$\frac{1}{2}$ cup = 125 mL
$\frac{2}{3}$ cup = 150 mL
$\frac{3}{4}$ cup = 175 mL
1 cup = 250 mL
2 cups = 1 pint = 500 mL
3 cups = 750 mL
4 cups = 1 quart = 1 L

VOLUME MEASUREMENTS (fluid)

1 fluid ounce (2 tablespoons) = 30 mL
4 fluid ounces ($\frac{1}{2}$ cup) = 125 mL
8 fluid ounces (1 cup) = 250 mL
12 fluid ounces (1$\frac{1}{2}$ cups) = 375 mL
16 fluid ounces (2 cups) = 500 mL

WEIGHTS (mass)

$\frac{1}{2}$ ounce = 15 g
1 ounce = 30 g
3 ounces = 90 g
4 ounces = 120 g
8 ounces = 225 g
10 ounces = 285 g
12 ounces = 360 g
16 ounces = 1 pound = 450 g

DIMENSIONS

$\frac{1}{16}$ inch = 2 mm
$\frac{1}{8}$ inch = 3 mm
$\frac{1}{4}$ inch = 6 mm
$\frac{1}{2}$ inch = 1.5 cm
$\frac{3}{4}$ inch = 2 cm
1 inch = 2.5 cm

OVEN TEMPERATURES

250°F = 120°C
275°F = 140°C
300°F = 150°C
325°F = 160°C
350°F = 180°C
375°F = 190°C
400°F = 200°C
425°F = 220°C
450°F = 230°C

BAKING PAN SIZES

Utensil	Size in Inches/Quarts	Metric Volume	Size in Centimeters
Baking or Cake Pan (square or rectangular)	8 × 8 × 2	2 L	20 × 20 × 5
	9 × 9 × 2	2.5 L	23 × 23 × 5
	12 × 8 × 2	3 L	30 × 20 × 5
	13 × 9 × 2	3.5 L	33 × 23 × 5
Loaf Pan	8 × 4 × 3	1.5 L	20 × 10 × 7
	9 × 5 × 3	2 L	23 × 13 × 7
Round Layer Cake Pan	8 × 1½	1.2 L	20 × 4
	9 × 1½	1.5 L	23 × 4
Pie Plate	8 × 1¼	750 mL	20 × 3
	9 × 1¼	1 L	23 × 3
Baking Dish or Casserole	1 quart	1 L	—
	1½ quart	1.5 L	—
	2 quart	2 L	—